Fontenay

Abbey

Julien Frizot

Editions Gaud

GENESIS

Leaving the highway and heading into the lush foliage of the forest of Fontenay, the visitor realises that he has come to a place unlike any other, to an image of the Heavenly City on Earth, an architectural masterpiece of the highest order classified by UNESCO in 1981 as a part of the World's Heritage.

IN THE BEGINNING WAS NATURE

There is a slight chill in the air. A light breeze ruffles the leaves of the forest which, as far as the eye can see, covers the Montbard plateau. Water is everywhere, penetrating into every nook and cranny of nature, here seemingly abandoned by man. Nevertheless, the region is far from being one of those deserted places in which Cistercians liked to set up their establishments. Contact point between the kingdom's great lords; the valley of Fontenay belongs to the lands of the Duke of Burgundy, Eudes II. The presence of the Church is evident everywhere; a few leagues away, in the village of Touillon, the Bishops of Autun, to whom the land of the Montbardois belonged, had a small château built as a summer residence. In a more local context, the land belongs to Raynard de Montbard, an uncle of Bernard de Clairvaux on his mother's side.

Bull of Pope Alexander III dating from 1168. It confirms the abbey's possessions and privileges.

Preceding page : letter F (Bibliothèque nationale, Latin ms. 2436, fol. 84 r°).

Bull of Pope Alexander III - Extract

« We furthermore command that apart from all possessions and all goods which the monastery at present holds justly and canonically or which it may acquire in the future through the favour of the Lord or by the grant of Supreme Pontiffs, the generosity of kings or princes, offerings of the faithful and by other just means, shall remain whole and intact in your possession or that of your successors »

Thus, when the latter decides to build a new religious establishment in the region, he appeals to family generosity and to the gratitude of Étienne de Bagé, the Bishop of Autun.

MEN OF GOOD WILL

In these circumstances, St. Bernard receives a first plot of land – placed by some historians on the plateau and by others at the bottom of the valley – and on which all members of the new community begin the work of reclamation. However, the growing success of this first new-born establishment compels Geoffroy de Roche-Vanneau, an uncle of Bernard and the first abbot of the new abbey, to request a new site.

The chosen place is not far away, at the intersection of the Combe Noire, through which a small stream flows, and of another small valley, crossed by a meandering brook.

This is, however, of little importance. Work is begun to rid the place of stagnant water and to tame the small watercourse; it is necessary to drain and drain again and to construct two embankments in order to reclaim the land. The first is built in the north, damming the Combe of Saint-Bernard. Over 35 metres long, it reaches in places a width of 23.5 metres and a height of 5 metres, forming a small pond, whose emptying to this day regulated by a duct supplying a channel which disappears within the abbey.

The second one, larger still, starts on the side of the valley and extends over 80 metres, its width reaching 2 meters and its height, a bit less, reaching 4.5 metres. The water of the brook is then diverted towards the south, protecting the abbey from possible flooding. Such is the huge volume of work which precedes the building of the abbey, because, before building the walls, it is also necessary to construct numerous new works for the supply clean water and the evacuation wastewater.

In order to erect buildings, the monks very probably enlist the help of artisans, skilled workmen and unskilled labourers, because the task is gigantic and complex. Some of them will join the community as lay brothers

t. Bernard's pond located north of the abbey.

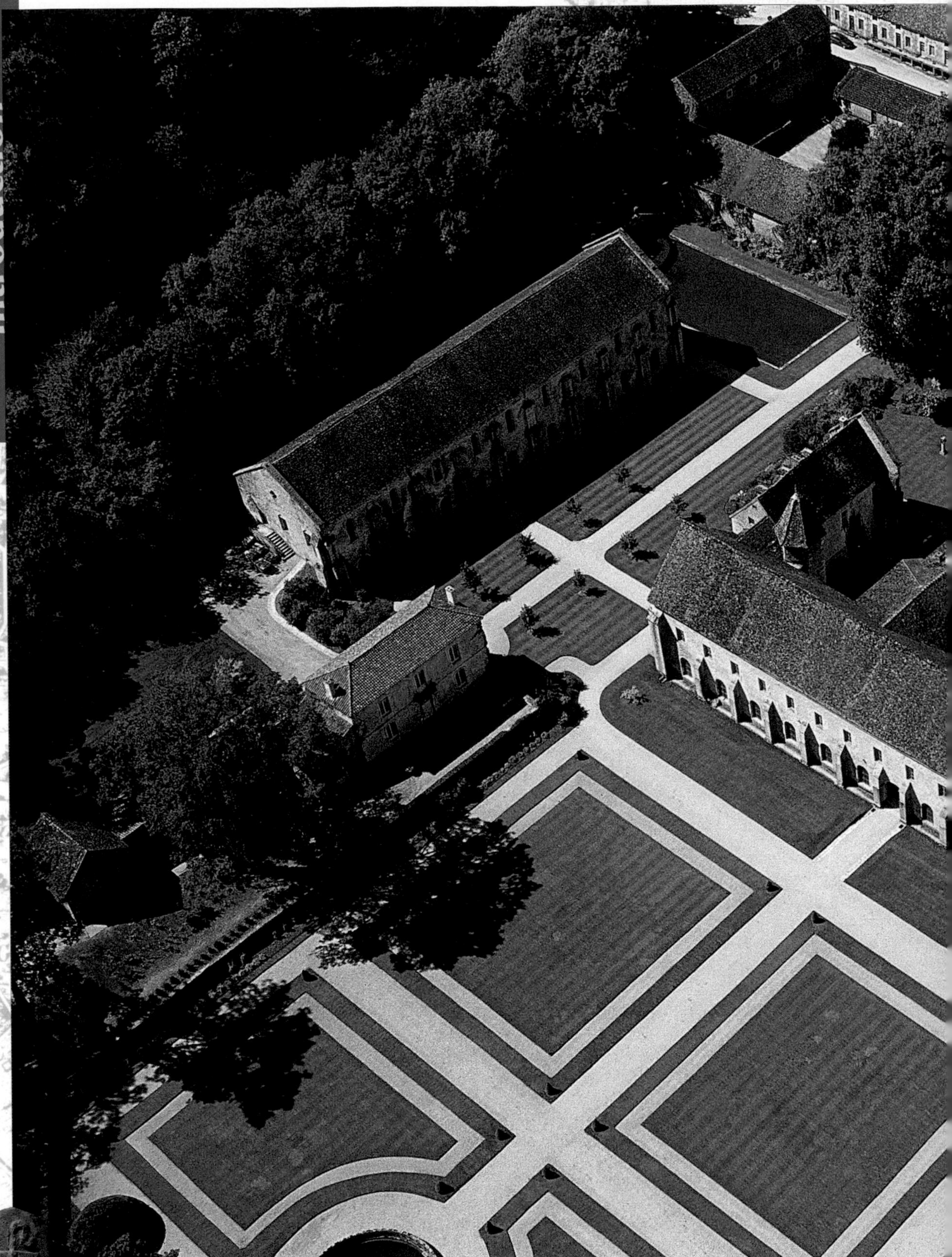

CISTERCIAN ARCHITECTURE?

REJECTION OF THE SUPERFLUOUS

Since the rules of the Order reject any sculptures or decorations in their abbeys, the architecture itself becomes the favoured area of expressing Cistercian art.

Being an expression of the rejection of triumphal art favoured by others, this art cannot exist for its own sake only, but rather as a convergence – expressed differently according to the region where the Cistercian order is present – of functional necessities, of its most rigid ideals and its spiritual aspirations which are most marked by austerity.

« We prohibit sculptures or paintings in our churches and in other parts of the monastery, because when one looks at them, one often neglects the need for meditation and the discipline of religious gravity », stresses a text, which expresses the will of the general council of the chapter in 1150.

These requirements surely sum up the Cistercian ideal, the demand for an architecture devoid of everything that is superfluous and one in which the human soul can expand without constraints or earthly references, so as the better to approach God.

ROMANESQUE AND GOTHIC

The Cistercians return to the most fundamental architectural elements, creating a hierarchy of forms and techniques, in order the better to give concrete expression to their ideal.

A high Gothic pointed barrel-vault surmounting the nave of the Fontenay church is an extreme symbol of the desire to strip the structure of any ornamentation.

In the chapter-house, these vaults, resting on intersecting ribs, illustrate the monks' mastery of this emergent style, which brings lightness and elevation to mediæval architecture.

Nevertheless, the Order does not adopt this new style to excess ; what appears superfluous in Gothic art is, at least at the beginning of its use, irremediably cast aside. Thus, the facade of the Cistercian church has several doors including small secondary openings, just when the central portal with its mass of sculptures, arches and other decorative frescoes in contemporary churches was expanding. The circular ground plan of an apse with radiating chapels and an ambulatory which are adopted by the large Cluniac abbeys and early cathedrals is abandoned in favour of an apse with chapels along the flat wall, such as may be seen at Fontenay.

Like the spiritual renewal which the order endeavours to inspire, the architecture developed by the Cistercians becomes a clear reaction against contemporary art. Spiritual and architectural ideals only seek to ensure that every architectural element illustrates some virtue and value of the Cistercian spirit, namely, modesty, morality and contemplation.

From top to bottom: the apse of the abbey church, the south aisle, a vault keystone in the chapter-house.

THE MAGIC OF PROPORTIONS

Modest and rigorous in terms of its decorations, Cistercian art also remains such as far as the proportions of buildings are concerned. In their quest, the Cistercian monks indeed favour harmonious proportions, the square and the simplest of curves. Everything is visualised and studied with a real concern to find the right measurements, the perfect balance and æsthetic design. To help them in their task, the monks resorted to the « golden number », whose calculation makes use of the following equation : $(1 + \sqrt{5})/2 = 1,61803$.

LIGHT

Light in Cistercian architecture is present in all its purity, a representation of the Most High. It decorates and trims the nave, taking the place of painting and sculpture. It plays with itself but also with shadow as it glides, as the day moves on, over the pillars of the nave and over the faces of the Virgin and Child, to disappear with the approach of twilight in the galleries of the cloister.

When the sun has gone and the walls are thickening, the vault which surmounts the nave appears to grow heavier, the walls come closer to one another ; darkness overtakes light, a propitious time for meditation. The clouds disperse and the light flashes again, penetrating the darkness of an aisle with its rays, bathing the apse in a soft light, soothing and uplifting in turn, a time for prayer.

In short, Cistercian art and its manner of ordering space reflect the soul of the monks and their way of ordering the spirit.

Double capital in the cloister.

In the church, the light, gliding along the stone up to the last hours of daylight, plays on the materials.

The church apse
In the XIIIth century
the semicircular
arches of the upper
triplet were converted
into triangular arches

The nave vault
rises to 16.70 m.

general council of the chapter of the order, ever increasing numbers of benefactors and those making generous donations prevailed upon the monks to let them be buried in the abbey church.

These prohibitions suffered the fate that is suffered by man, i.e., they are there for but a moment. Was not the floor of the church paved with coloured tiles whilst the *Apology* of St. Bernard condemns any ostentatious paving decoration as well as painting or sculpture? Some rediscovered vestiges of this paving are presented in the choir.

This fact will not escape a visitor who, on arrival in the choir, turns round towards the entrance of the church; the building receives a disturbing light which diffuses through the facade, the apse and the chancel. The upper part of the facade is pierced by seven windows, a symbolic number, arranged in two rows. The apse and the transept ribs are bathed in light diffused by the eleven openings made in the apse and the back wall of the crossing.

The roof of the church is devoid of a roof frame; above the nave vault, a block foundation extends over the entire length of the building, being itself covered by a bond of stones on which the small warm coloured round tiles are laid.

The holy of holies, the square church choir in the purest Cistercian tradition is raised by two steps and bathed in a soft light diffused by two rows of windows arranged in sets of three. It too is surmounted by a pointed Gothic barrel-vault, but a much lower one than that surmounting the nave. This difference of level is offset by a bottom wall, which rises above the triumphal arch and is pierced by five storied openings.

Southern elevation of the nave seen from the transept crossing. Above the door, seven windows – a symbolic number – diffuse light at sunset.

...e five openings in the semicircular arch of the triumphal wall are ...additional source of light in a nave devoid of high windows.

The Virgin and Child

The first rays of the sun pouring through the three choir windows, symbols of the Trinity, bathe the Virgin-Mother, the Patron of the abbey, in a soft light. Her face lights up in a charming smile, the smile of a mother with a grave bearing, playing with her child. Her right leg is slightly bent, her weight gracefully shifted to the other, her head delicately crowned and her body enveloped in a long robe, Mary carries the Child on her right arm. His right arm is held round his mother's neck, his other hand holding a dove with outspread wings against his chest.

The Virgin's right hand, today broken, formerly held a sceptre. Dating from the XIIth century, this statue was for a long time exposed to the weather in the cemetery of the neighbouring community of Touillon. Following restoration, this admirable figure found a place worthy of its beauty, but it has lost its polychrome tones, even though, on some folds of her mantle, traces of blue are still detectable.

Interior view of the north transept chapels. In the original building, the two chapels did not communicate with one another. The break-through the partition separating them was made in the XIVth centu...

14

ke the rest of the furnishings, the church altars have disappeared.
the south corner of the choir, a rectangular font has been dug
to the thickness of the wall. The church stalls could not withstand
andalism and humidity which forced the monks, around 1750, to
ise the church floor by almost a metre. On either side of a mo-
ic consisting of the most recent tiles to be discovered in the
oisters, set in the floor, the memorial stones of great lords and of
ominent ecclesiastics are on display.

*Interior view of the south transept chapels.
On the left is the tomb of the Seigneurs de Mello.*

*Exterior view of one
of one of the south
transept chapels.
Not long ago, the
roof of these chapels
was a single pitch
roof. It has been
restored to its
original form.*

ew of the row of choir chapels. Notwithstanding the repeated prohibition of the general
apter council in the XIIth and XIIIth centuries, benefactors rapidly secured the right
be buried in the abbey church, like the Seigneurs de Mello in the XIVth century.

The north aisle of the churh.

The Sacristy

At the end of the south transept behind the staircase which runs along the wall and leads to the monks' dormitory, open two doors; the one on the right, now walled up, dates from 1760, the one on the left leads to the sacristy, the *vestiarium* of ancient texts, which, judging from the traces which appear on the floor, was probably separated from the huge hall by a small partition. Surmounted by a vault on intersecting ribs, it's architecture is similar to that of the chapterhouse with which it communicates.

In a Cistercian abbey, the sacristy is not in any sense a place overflowing with richly decorated objects because, as the Order states, « the use of a gold cross shall be forbidden and a wooden cross shall be used; a single candelabra shall suffice… the censers shall be of copper or iron, the chasubles of hemp, flax or wool without gold or silver embroidery… the chalices shall no longer be of gold, but of silver or enamel… the altar cloth shall be of linen, without any decoration » (*Capitula*, XXV,2 and XXVI,2).

The sacristy vault was rebuilt in the middle of the XVth century, after the fire in the dormitory above.

View of the north transept. At its entrance sits enthroned the graceful statue of the Virgin and Child, lit up by the double triplet of the apse.

As far as the church transepts are concerned, they have two points in common with the choir; they are surmounted by a Gothic pointed barrel-vault and are less high than the nave.

Two rectangular chapels surmounted by a Gothic pointed barrel-vault lit by a window and connected with one another by semi-circular arches are both open to the east.

Whilst in the centre of the north transept, pierced by the « door of the dead » through which deceased monks were carried to the cemetery, a graceful statue of the Virgin and Child is enthroned (see box on page 14), the south transept houses more discreetly a tomb with the remains of the Seigneur de Mello and his wife, abbey benefactors of the end of the XIVth century. With a nave skirted by two side aisles, a transept flanked by four chapels pointing east and a choir with a flat apse, the Fontenay abbey church adopts the typical Order ground plan found in Cistercian churches from Portugal to Scandinavia.

17

THE CLOISTER

The engraved decoration of certain cloister pilasters (detail).

A FOUNTAIN OF LIGHT

The church is the soul of the abbey, the cloister its heart, a heart which cannot find a place elsewhere than under the left wing of this church, opening on to a square of blue sky.

Cross-roads of the universe, a city of God, a mirror of man, the cloister diffuses the light from on high through the openings in its bays which mark the tempo -like the prayers in the lives of the monks- of the galleries which surround these fountains of astonishing serenity. A closed space touched by divine grace, it diffuses the mystery of creation from its four sides and evokes the garden of paradise « where flows a stream of spring water which divides into four channels ». In this place, all things are dispersed and come together again and are but one around the Light of Heaven.

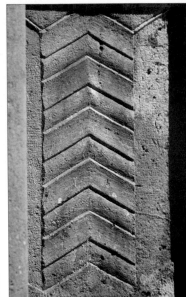

THE CROSS-ROADS

The life of the monastery revolves round the cloister and it is in this space that the monks and lay brothers pass one another, each occupied with his own spiritual or temporal concerns.

The different abbey buildings are grouped around its galleries.

Firstly, the east gallery, which is by far the most frequented, serves rooms which are reserved for spiritual activity ; directly adjoining the church nave it takes the monks from the choir to the services, but also, at the end of the morning service, to the chapter-house for a reading of the Rule. At its southern end, a staircase leads to the monks' dormitory.

There, the precentor who is responsible for abbey works, comes to open the armarium set in the wall. Behind the heavy wooden shutters lie valuable commentaries on the psalms or other works of hagiography which some of the monks read aloud whilst walking along the galleries, particularly the north gallery known as the « *collatio* ». In this gallery which adjoins the church, the monks sit, waiting to hear the reading which precedes the service of compline. According to certain historians, this is also where the mandatum, the washing of the feet, was practised, a reminder of the duty of humility and charity towards one's neighbour, whether he is a member of the community or otherwise.

Most of the activities linked to the use of water ta place in the gallery opposite, on the south side close the washbasin, the refectory gallery. This gallery had t special function of accommodating, in an excrescen on the courtyard side, a washbasin opposite the refe tory door. According to other historians, as it is nat rally close to the spring, the mandatum, the washing the feet mentioned earlier, took place there.

This gallery serves the calefactory and the abbey k chens, as does the western gallery.

Above, the northeast corner of the cloister.

Cloister openings. Some tympani surmounting the twin arches are pierced with small oculi.

s the centre of monastery life, the cloister exhibits a ertain amount of activity, particularly when bad weather revents the monks from leaving the abbey to work in e fields. During the hours of rest, and particularly after e midday meal, the monks may walk there in silence. this cloister also take place processions preceded by e crucifix; the monks progress in two rows enveloped their ample choir cowls and followed by the lay bro-

thers. Crucifix in hand, the abbot, escorted by the prior and the cellarer, closes the procession.

Sometimes joining the procession are distinguished guests, nobles and knights attending the interment of one of their own kind who has secured the favour – a sign of a relaxation of the Rule – of resting eternally in the abbey nave and benefiting from the eternal prayers of the monks.

A well of light, the cloister floods the heart of abbey with a warm presen
More pragmatically, each gallery had its own function: the north gallery is used for mea
the south gallery for daily life, the east gallery accommodates rooms used for abbey managemen

REMARKABLE ARCHITECTURE

The spiritual and decision-making centre of the community, the chapter-house is the object of every care during its building and is often of generous proportions.

At Fontenay, the chapter-house opens on the east gallery of the cloister through a large archway supported by four tori of the archivolt, which rest against an equal number of small columns. The capitals and the bases of these columns are in every respect identical with those of the galleries.

On either side of this wide opening is a double semicircular opening, also flanked by small columns, fully opening on the cloister. Apart from its functional aspect, i.e., allowing lay brothers to be present at the daily reading of some chapters from the Rule, these openings illustrate other aspects of the Cistercian spirit, the spirit of transparency and of openness to the world.

Originally, this chapter-house comprised three wide bays surmounted by vaults on intersecting ribs which were as long as they were wide. It was, accordingly, completely square.

The six vaults still standing are supported by transverse arches which, in turn, rest on wide groups of columns surrounding a central core. Standing alone in the middle of chapter-house, two pillars support the weight of the ceiling and of the monks' dormitory above. Between an octagonal abacus and the tiled floor of the room, these pillars, which consist of small shafts of columns are decorated with graceful, very simple capitals, but nevertheless ornamented with veined Gothic leaves.

The keystones are delicately decorated with flowers, all different from one another. At the bottom of the arches set against the walls, there are no corbels to distribute the weight among the walls, but solid half-pillars, resting on a large base against the wall.

At the top: several dozen joint mark
appear on the abbey stone
Above: a superb intersection of vault rib

Menology

The Fontenay calendar. Two commemorations had to be solemnly read at the Chapter council on January 11 th and on December 20 th. The second begins as follows:

« On the 3rd of the Ides de January, the following commemoration shall be read: for the Supreme Pontiff, Dom Guillaume, 2nd abbot of Fontenay; for Dom Arnaud, 3rd abbot of Fontenay; for Dom Bernard, formerly abbot of Fontenay, later general of Cîteaux; for Dom Martin, and for all the departed bishops and abbots of our order; for Henry, King of England, for Count Thibaut and his son and for Richard, King of England.
On the 4 th of the Calends of February, for the death of Helvidia or Elisa or Hila, the Lady of Époisses
On the 8 th of the Calends of March, for the death of William, Lord of Époisses (1326)
On the 4 th of the Calends of March, for the death of Roger de Mortemart, Count of Marche
On the 15 th of the Calends of April, for the birthday of Pope Honorius
On the 6 th of the Calends of April, for the death of Robert, Duke of Burgundy
On the 12 th of the Calends of June, for the death of Etienne, Bishop of Autun
On the 11 th of the Calends of September, for the death of Eustachie de Mellot
On the 4 th of the Ides of October, for the death of Ebrard, Bishop of Norwich
On the 16 th of the Calends of November, for the death of de Robert, Count of Tonnerre
On the 12 th of the Calends of November, for the death of Etienne, Bishop of Autun
On the 7 th of the Calends of December, for the birthday of Jean d'Époisses
On the Nones of December, for the birthday of Jeanne, Countess of Flanders
On the 8 th of the Ides of December, for the death of Hugues, Bishop of Auxerre
On the 19 th of the Calends of January, for the birthday of Queen Berengaria and her sister, Countess of Champagne. »

This break-through of the partition separating the chapter-house and the visiting room dates from the beginning of the XXth century. It is an enlargement of the first opening dating from the XIXth century.

Little indication remains as to how this room was furnished. In other chapter-houses, the floor has retained traces of the position of stone benches. At Fontenay, only some conjectures as to the use of wooden benches give some of the answers. The benches running along the north and south walls of the room, as is the case in the locutory, do not really permit making any general inferences.

The Passage to the Garden

Between the visiting room and the great hall is a wide passage which connects, at the intersection of the south and east galleries, the garden and the cloister.

The two side passageways were broken through at the beginning of the 20th century

Wide cluster of small columns at the entrance to the chapter-house.

The Visiting Room

Before all else, pragmatism prevails in a monastery; it is this pragmatism which determines the necessities of monastic life, reduced to their simplest expression. Thus, small as it may be, every room has its purpose and its importance.

Far from being spacious, the visiting room is nevertheless a strategic area of the abbey; it is in fact where the prior spends his time. At the end of each daily chapter meeting, it is here that he receives monks, speaks to each of them individually or in small groups, ordering and confirming to each his work for the day.

It is also in the visiting room that the master of novices speaks with every new arrival in order to facilitate his first steps within the community.

Of modest appearance, the visiting room at present appears to be open to the four winds. This does not take into account the architectural changes occurring in this east wing of the abbey, first and foremost of which is the disappearance of the third bay. Destroyed by fire around 1450, this bay gave greater cohesion to the chapter-house and the sacristy. To this are added modifications made at the time of the restoration of the building. At Fontenay, the break-through for the door giving on the corridor – leading from the cloister to the medicinal herb garden – was not made until later, as in the case of the

Subtle refinement in the visiting room; as in the chapter-house, the vault keystones are decorated with floral motifs.

partition which still partly separates the chapter-house from the visiting room.

The original visiting room must be imagined as an enclosed space, a small, long room, with a door opening on the cloister on the west side, and with a wide window on the east side. For this reason, and in contrast with the notion of openness and transparency, this is undoubtedly the only room which the monks are forbidden to enter without being invited to do so.

As far as its architecture is concerned, here the treatment is identical with that of the chapter-house, sharing with it both luminosity with its large picture window, and a concern for detail, as evidenced by the flowers decorating its two vault keystones.

THE DORMITORY

The Bell Turret

Above the dormitory, at the summit of the east wing of the cloister, the dormitory bell-tower has found its place. Here at Fontenay, there is no need for a bell-tower at the crossing of the transept to call the flock to mass, but only a bell turret to mark the rhythm of the day, punctuated by services. This modest construction complies with prescriptions limiting bell turret size and issued by the general chapter of the order in 1157. Of the two small bells which formerly hung one above the other, only one, connected by means of a long rope to the monks' common room, now remains.

On the west facade of this bell turret, engraved in the stone, appear the arms of the abbey « gules with three gold bands and two bars, crowned and surmounted by a gold fleur-de-lys ».

A flight of steps leads to the monks' dormitory. Devoid of a partition wall and bathed in a strong light, this huge room above the chapter-house and the monks' common room occupies the entire length of the east building. Formerly, it was lit at sunset by fourteen narrow, arched openings which were discovered under the plastering and brought to light. On the wall which opens east on the French-style park, three great arches discovered under the wall parge-work show that the dormitory extended above the bay of the chapter-house which is now demolished, forming an annexe which was undoub-

tedly reserved for the abbot – who alon had the right to separate himself from th rest of the monks – or for other dignitarie: Latrines adjoined the dormitory; pipes hav been found which led to a channel from th river and which passes beneath the monk common room located on the ground floc Originally, it was undoubtedly surmounte by a pointed Gothic arch barrel-vault whic presumably collapsed following a fire in th XVth century and was replaced by an ama zing oak frame which, to this day, is in a pe fect state of preservation.

Chapter XXII of the *Rule of St. Benedict* r quires the monks to share the same dorm tory, without a fire or excessive light, to slee on straw mats on the floor and not in sm. individual cells then allowed by other orde Only two rows of simple low wooden part tions with a central corridor allowing supe

The monks' dormitory with its narrow windows, on the first floor of the east wing.

View, from the French garden, of the dormito which occupies the entire floor of the monks' buildi

...ision, separate the monks from each other.
...ater, straw mat give way to small, slightly
...aised beds and low partitions to real walls.
...Although certain Cistercian abbey dormito–
...es such as those at Sénanque still show on
...he floor imprints of these stalls installed in
...he huge room, Fontenay has preserved no
...ace of them.

...he monks sleep fully dressed under a sheet
...nd a woollen blanket, ready to rise in order
...o attend vigil services before sunrise. With
...yes still heavy with sleep, the monks silently
...escend into the church by the staircase
...which leads to the south cruciform portion.
...n daytime, the dormitory is nevertheless not
...a closed room; the monks being able to go
...here, particularly during summer months,
...or a short rest.

*In the XIIth century, a first staircase of
twenty-seven steps led to the church.
In the XVIIIth century, with the raising of the
nave floor, another staircase of twenty-four
steps was built.
It was extended by five steps at the beginning of
the XXth century when the church floor was
brought back down to its original level.*

A Monk's Personal Affairs

A monk must be able to content himself with a minimum of possessions.
Thus, his clothes will be few and
cheap.
None may have more than two tunics
and two cowls, the wearing of body
linen being allowed only when travel-
ling, a belt (the *cingulum*), a scapular
for work, as well as stockings and two
pairs of shoes.
Every monk is responsible for his
straw mattress and the bowl from
which he eats his meals. Less restricted than the monks to rigour of dress,
the lay brothers will be provided with
coarse brown tunics.
The nuns of the order shall wear a veil
– black for those who have taken their
vows and white for novices and lay
sisters – a garment which will confer
on them the title of brides of Christ.

Detail of the three arcades proving that the dormitory extended eastward prior to the fire in 1450.

View to the south of the monks' dormitory, covered with a superb wooden roof frame.

THE MONKS' COMMON ROOM

South gable of the monks' building. On the ground floor, the monks' common room entrance doors. The triplet of the monks' dormitory on the upper floor.

In the south of the east wing, in the extension of the chapter-house, of the small locutory and the passage which connects the cloister to the gardens there opens a 30-metre long room, surmounted by twelve ribbed vaults forming six bays.

What was its purpose? Some have thought it was the abbey store room or at least its provisions store, but it appears difficult to admit any such use; such huge store rooms for food-stuffs which are subject to constant movement of provisions of every kind in the immediate vicinity of the chapter-house! In many Cistercian abbeys, it was the custom to build the store room at right angles to the church, opposite the cloister and outside the premises reserved for the monks.

Some believed that they have identified the scriptorium, the famous room in which monastic copyists were employed on the lengthy and meticulous copying of manuscripts. Other speak of a room where members of the choir and lay brothers devote themselves to the work of repairs, to hairdressing and other day-to-day tasks, far removed from liturgic concerns.

But why force the different rooms of an abbey into a r ductive schema as rigid as the Rule of St. Benedict?

Freed from that logic, the Fontenay abbey monks' cor mon room is without a doubt more of a room for diff rent uses, than a mere scriptorium. The work of the m nastic copyists requires good, preferably natural, lightir provided here by six wide openings. This activity also ca for deep silence, to enable them to concentrate on the task.

View to the south. The huge room is divided into two naves by a spine of massive pillars.

Cistercian monks appear to be ingenious and inventive in making simple movable wooden partitions which would have enabled the copyists to separate themselves from noise, in order to allow them the better to concentrate on their work along the bays on the side of the openings. When the days shorten on arrival of winter, when the chorister-monks and lay brothers cannot continue working outside and when the copyists cannot continue their exacting work, the writing tables and movable partitions are pushed into a corner of the room and the community now peacefully devotes itself to reading, to petty tasks and to pottering about as on bad-weather days and especially when the calefactory is close by.

The architecture of the monks' common room is reminiscent of the chapter-house with which it is coæval, though it is neither as elegant nor as light.

Along the 30 metre long axis of the room, five powerful columns – the central one of which differs from the rest in having an octagonal shaft – support the spring of the pointed arches and beams which support the twelve vaults.

Unlike those in the chapter-house, these arches and beams rest against the walls on large corbels in the shape of inverted pyramids, ending in a flower bud, a form quite common in Burgundy.

Its austerity notwithstanding, this room is nevertheless also discreetly decorated with floral motifs analogous to those in the chapter-house which enliven the intersecting ribs. Indeed, finely worked sculptures decorate the bases of the arches at the level of the entablature; roses and floral motifs add an artistic note to column capitals.

In the south, the monks' common room gives on the garden, on the west, on the courtyard formed by the infirmary, but most importantly, on the calefactory.

Lieux de vie

Cistercian Illuminations

Defined by the statutes as « a monk's treasure », books are given every attention. It is even mandatory for every abbey to possess certain titles to be kept in the *armarium*.
The reproduction of these books which deteriorate with age and which are often lent by one community to another, is the long and exacting task of the monastic copyists.

This activity of copyist requires a great deal equipment, writing tables, pens and knives for sharpening them, inkwells, rulers, styli and wax tablets… In addition to this equipment, various colours, coloured inks and gold leaf, are needed for the execution of richly illuminated initials.
It is with reference these initials that doubts and discussions arise. In the Cistercian world, the statutes prescribe a uniformity of style for all abbeys. Nevertheless, the first period of the work of illumination shows an extraordinary degree of diversity, both as to colour and to form. Even human forms, always in a posture complying with the principles, appear in some illuminated initials *(Moralia in Job)*.
Already, however, oriental (Byzantine) influences begin to appear in the illuminations. This period of ostentation – considered by some as very far removed from St. Benedict's rules of humility and simplicity – becomes toned down with the end of the abbacy of Stephen Harding (1109-1133).
Under the influence of Bernard de Clairvaux, the original asceticism is now applied to the work of the copyists. A purified and simplified style is imposed and with it a monochrome and bare design. The agents of this change are the monks of Clairvaux, often itinerant monks and who are to be found at numerous abbeys where they promote the reforming zeal of St. Bernard.
Nevertheless, this austerity only lasts for a certain length time. As early as the beginning of the XIIIth century, figurative forms with gold reappear, accompanied by human forms. In the towns, the production of manuscripts is growing. A luxury craft of book manufacture is spreading, gradually inducing the monks to entrust the work of illumination to craftsmen outside the monastery.
By the XVth century, the abbeys are purchasing the majority of the works that they require.

Letter S with filigree and antennæ.
(Bibliothèque nationale,
Latin ms. 2436, fol. 83 v°).

Vault keystones with a stylised motif.

The monks' common room is a 30-metre long hall spanned by six bays with intersecting vault ribs.

THE MEDICINAL HERB GARDEN

EXPERIENCE AND DEVELOPMENT OF A PLANT HERITAGE

Monasteries had managed, during the stormy epochs which followed the fall of the Western Roman empire, to safeguard the essentials of their knowledge
In this context, the garden, a basic source of the monks' food, received from them the most attentive and meticulous care.
The oldest list of plants grown in our regions is that in the ordinance of Charlemagne, called the *De Villis* ordinance, enacted in about 795. In addition to mentioning almost ninety species of plant then under cultivation, it specifies the existence of four « gardens » in every monastery. Two are purely utilitarian, the vegetable garden and the herb garden, the famous medicinal herb garden, where medicinal plants are cultivated. The third, the cemetery, lies between two worlds ; the rows of tombs reposing beneath the green grass, token of future happiness, whilst the rows of trees symbolise resurrection. Lastly, the cloister garden at the cross-roads of the four axes of the world and at the centre of the monastery is, on the other hand, symbolic.
From the Mediterranean countries (Italy, Spain or even the Byzantine empire), new species of plants appear in our regions and become acclimatised, joining the vegetables, the medicinal plants, flowers and fruit trees already under cultivation. A very

active communications network, source of frequent and fruitful exchanges, exists among monasteries. Ideas, news, but also goods of every kind, including cuttings, seeds and other plants developed in their turn at monasteries, circulate…
Mediæval knowledge thus often goes beyond the confines of gardens, whether vegetable or medicinal herb gardens ; numerous wild plants, common in the surrounding countryside, are cultivated for the preparation of remedies, others are picked to supplement or to replace food.
Mediæval medicinal herb gardens could only hold a limited number of plants, each in a quantity sufficient to cover everyday needs. In general, only rare plants or plants foreign to the region are cultivated with the greatest care.

PRINCIPLES OF HERBALISM

At Fontenay abbey, the medicinal herb garden, which has today disappeared, was close to the infirmary in front of the novices' hall, on the site of the present French garden.

In the immediate vicinity, were vegetable gardens and the small orchards needed for domestic use.

The monks, helped by the lay brothers or by farm labourers, carefully follow the calendar of the growth and the flowering of plants, divided into beds and separated by alleyways; the gathering of the flowers is carried out at the beginning of the flowering season or when they are in full bloom.

Drying processes make it possible to preserve the active components of these plants. Most often, plants are dried in the shade, hung in a bunch far from any source of smoke and humidity. This drying is not, however, suited to all plants; many of them lose their virtue on drying (borage, cress, orchis, sempervivum…). Such plants must accordingly be used fresh.

Ornamental plants are also seen as medicinal plants. The benefit which is derived from them resides solely in their beauty.

The Infirmary

In compliance with the Rule of St. Benedict and with the statutes drawn up by the Cistercian order, the infirmary is systematically isolated for reasons of hygiene. Located well away from the principal abbey buildings, not far from the river, the Fontenay infirmary is built facing east.

Along with the kitchen and the calefactory, the infirmary has a fireplace in which logs are burned for the comfort of the sick monks. Otherwise, there is no unnecessary luxury; sick and weakened monks spend a minimum time at the infirmary. They have a right to two or three days of eating meat so as to recover their strength before returning to the community.

As regards its architecture, although the walls appear to go back to the foundation of the abbey, the openings are of a later date. The northern facade of the building, moreover, shows traces of former curved lintels.

Inside the infirmary, a handsome Louis XIII staircase exhibits a superb wrought iron banister.

47

WATER

The water of St. Bernard's brook where it enters the perimeter of the abbey. Tamed and under control, it illustrates the work o the monks to canalise the water in the vall

HYDRAULICS AT FONTENAY

Contrary to what is generally thought, with regard to hydraulics, innovation has a lesser presence than pragmatics in Cistercian works. No major technical innovation, no technological revolution appears to originate with the Cistercians but rather an ability for sharp observation, an incomparable persistence in developing sites where water is plentiful.

At Fontenay, at the meeting point of a combe and of a valley, the abbey is protected behind two high embankments which make it possible to tame the flow entering into the abbey enclosure. It is, however, still necessary to distribute the water for the community's domestic and sanitary needs…

WATERCOURSES

Thirty years elapsed between the arrival of St. Bernard and the consecration of the abbey church. During this period the monks carried out the huge task of drainage.

Their system included not only a se of open channels, but most impor tantly, an underground domesti supply and evacuation networ consisting of a large collector an adjoining galleries.

Built in the open prior to the erectio of the principal abbey buildings, consisted of terracotta or ston pipes. Its backbone was a covere barrel-shaped gallery, 1.35 metre wide and 1.40 to 1.90 metres hig with 0.60 metre high, reinforced pas sages under the building founda tions.

The weaker parts of this difficult-to-access networ not spared by the passing of time, were reinforce with the help of pillars, doubtless in the XVIIIth cer tury, when the last of the works were carried out. A most of the pipes were inaccessible, they will be abar doned by the monks who will have to raise the floo in order to avoid silting. Today, thanks to the pow of water which flushes it automatically, the princip system is still working.

The arrival of water within the monastery determine the general arrangement of the buildings around th church. The square of the cloister extends both nor and south of the nave, in the direction of the river. Th domestic buildings were built at a lower point, clo to the conduit of the collector connected to the riv At Fontenay, the principal collector skirts the outbu dings served by the south wing of the cloiste Crossing the monks and lay brothers' latrine, it ev cuates wastewater and collects rainwater via mason gullies.

One question remains. Who carried out the constru tion of such a network; the abbey monks, the lay br thers, paid labourers, or wandering monks? Only or thing is certain: when the Cistercians appeared at th beginning of the XIIth century, the communities, (v lages, market towns…) had long before already c verted rivers, built canals to drive mill wheels, and u dertaken the embankment of ponds.

The principal merit of the Cistercian monks with r gard to hydraulics resides less in their inventive ab lities, than in their spirit of pragmatism which adap to local hydrographic conditions.

Simplified plan of the hydraulic system circuit in the Middle Ages.

THE WASHBASIN

When a continuous supply of water to the washbasin was no longer possible, the monks demolished it. Only fragments of the vault wall ribs will remain.

ust as the monks are restricted to a very austere diet, cleanliness is a compulsory part of monastic life. Everyone must wash his hands before entering or leaving the refectory, as well as on returning from the fields and before entering the church. For this sole but symbolic purpose, every monastery possesses a covered washbasin. Of modest dimensions, it can be accommodated under the cloister galleries, but it is, most frequently, large and for this purpose a yard is built in an extension of the cloister, either in a corner, or in a kind of annexe adjoining the gallery which skirts the refectory.

At Fontenay, it was situated in a courtyard opposite the refectory entrance, as evidenced by the fragments of vault ribs which are still visible outside, at the angle of the gallery buttresses.

Built according to a square ground plan with two wide bays, this architectural annexe was supported by archways conforming in every detail to the latter. It was surmounted by four groined vaults whose springers were supported by a central column that passed through the large circular washbasin.

This basin, supplied by a pipe the traces of whose course are still detectable under the cloister paving, allowed water to escape through numerous tubulures pierced on its circumference, and thus allowed a large number of chorister-monks to wash at the same time. Excavations have uncovered all the foundations of the building. The pipe serving for the evacuation of wastewater still exists and corresponds exactly to the location of the washbasin. It flows into a waste canal, which runs beneath the large refectory.

The cloister washbasin according to a reconstitution by Viollet-le-Duc.

THE FORGE

The upper canal runs into the lower canal, to flow westwards.

During the second half of the XIIth century, the Fontenay monks erected a large forge within the precincts of the abbey in order to work ore.

Situated away from the monastic buildings on the banks of the canalised river, the building is nearly 53 metres long and 23.50 metres wide. As imposing as it is massive, it is reinforced by a row of two-tiered buttresses distributed evenly over the four facades.

Under its tiled roof, there is a row of four rooms separated by partition walls. The first, close to the washbasin, is undoubtedly the most elegant and the most « refined » of these four rooms. It is surmounted by four ribbed vaults, whose ribs rest along the walls on corbels and in clusters on a central column. The keystones of these vaults are decorated with small floral motifs as in the monks' common room and the chapter-house, a surprising aspect in a building which can be described as industrial.

Two large arches must have communicated with the next room, the forge proper. The latter must have been surmounted by a conical vault, built on pointed arches which reached to the top of the building. This vault, which no longer exists today, most likely ended in a skylight in order to improve ventilation. Only fragments of its vault ribs remain.

On the south wall, a hearth recreates the atmosphere of this production site. Along the side, it is still possible to see where a second hearth must have been, the beginning of its hood is still visible.

The third room, the largest in the building, has much in common with the chapter-house and the monks' common room. Like the former, it is surmounted by lofty ribbed vaults less massive and more airy than those in the monks' common room. As in the case of the latter, the ribs and the beams of these arches rest on imposing bases which in turn, rest on the walls and on the high capitals decorated with Gothic leaves. Three semicircular windows open on the river and two others in the opposite wall let in ample light, even though the lower part of each is obstructed.

The last room, known as the « mill room » is surmounted by four intersecting ribbed vaults and lit on the south side by two huge openings. It is there that the driving wheels must have been located, enclosed in a small side building borne by arches still standing, that span the watercourse. Nevertheless, this recital and apparent homogeneity give only a scant account of the development of the building: a study has brought to light several different phases of construction and of major modifications, occurring at different periods. From the epoch of its industrial functioning, the forge has preserved an imposing network of canals on two levels along the south facade to drive the water wheels which actuate the tilt hammers and the cupola* furnace bellows.

The lower canal dates for the Middle Ages. It consists of a now subterranean room supplied by a lateral water pipe from the canal and a covered conduit from the upper canal. This masonry canal is of XIXth

In the forge, a furnace recreates the ambience of this production site.

*Cupola furnace : crucible metal smelting furnace.

This forge room, the largest in the building, exhibits numerous similarities to the monks' common room: the ribs and the beams of these arches rest on imposing bases which, in turn, rest on the walls and on the high capitals decorated with Gothic leaves.

51

Ore

Pontigny, Auberive, Vauluisant but also Fontenay around 1140… From their very creation, abbeys launch iron smelting works so as to manufacture more easily the tools and instruments needed for their work.

Although the monks very often find themselves in competition with the lay lords of the region, those of Fontenay have the full support of the lords of Montbard, who grant to them the right to work the deposits of the neighbouring forests, particularly at Les Munières, a few hundred metres from the abbey. Nevertheless, these grants do not mean that the mine is accessible ; the right to work the ore has indeed been granted, but the vein remains to be discovered, to be developed and then to be worked.

Sometimes the ore outcrops. Lay brothers, paid servants or serfs now dig ditches most frequently strengthened by sawn timber and build huts to shelter the works. The extracted ore is finally cleaned before being smelted and then reduced. This stage of reduction develops with the appearance of hydraulic rams, which require, as is the case at Fontenay, the proximity of an abundant water supply.

Numerous disorders and the insecurity in the lower Middle Ages lead to a drop in iron smelting activity. Though blacksmiths are present at the abbey, supplies will have to be obtained form outside.

Map of Fontenay possessions in the Middle Ages.

The buttresses amplify the impression of power which the building conveys.

...entury origin. The water pipe draws directly, in a straight line, on the Fontenay watercourse.

...hese two mutually superimposed systems continue as far as the centre of the facade. ...here, the upper canal flows from a height ...f 2.6 metres into the lower canal, which extends in a westerly direction

...ONOPOLISTIC REASONING?

...n the beginning, the communities equip ...he abbey sites for internal consumption, ...ith a double supply network of drinking ...ater and of wastewater evacuation, which ...lso furnishes the energy required for the ...roper functioning of the abbey and its ...roduction. Very quickly, however, the ...onks try to secure the exclusive use of ...he watercourses in the area in which they ...ave settled, together with the rights atta-...ed thereto. As donations increase their ...mporalities and as the recognition of the ...cal nobility gives them a privileged status, ...e abbeys extend their influence upstream ...nd downstream. Thus, Fontenay has avai-...ble retting ponds and mills on the water-...ourses and founds fisheries whose pro-...cts are highly prized by the lords of the ...ngdom...

The Clientele

In the beginning, the monks contented themselves with manufacturing for abbey needs, but by the end of the XIIth century, the newly produced iron had become an important article of business with the world outside the abbey. The reason for this development was a surplus of production which the monks wanted to sell, without betraying the ideas of the Benedictine rule.

Increased demand was confronted with a shortage in supply. Taking advantage of the situation, the Cistercians produced more; investments which were still restricted and an embryonic competition earned them considerable profits. The conditions moreover proved favourable:

- the ore frequently outcropped and was therefore easy to extract;
- the iron content in the region was particularly high (sometimes almost 65 %), a prerequisite to limiting losses due to incomplete reduction.

Finally, accompanying this knowledge of ore was an extensive knowledge of hydraulics.

Édouard Aynard surrounded by his family.

The church nave converted into a warehouse for material used in the paper factory.

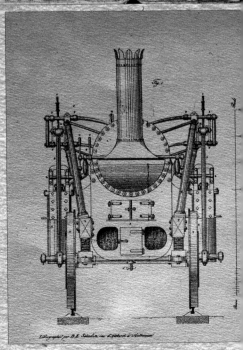

Front view of the engine of the railway line from Lyon to Saint-Étienne, pictured by Marc Seguin.

The Industrial Era

In 1820, Fontenay abbey becomes the property of Élie de Montgolfier, a well-known Annonay papermaker. The monks' work of iron smelting is succeeded by the manufacture of blotting paper and rag paper. The new activity naturally calls for new buildings; the valley bristles with tall chimneys and the ancient abbey buildings are converted into warehouses and material depots. The church soon receives a steam boiler. The cloister galleries are split up into workshop. Paper-sorting machines are installed in the chapter-house. Lastly, the forge gets a first floor and annexes are soon clinging to the thousand-year old walls.

The Cistercian abbey has become an industrial plant employing almost three hundred and sixty workers.

At the turn of the XXth century, this machine seizes up; the available hydraulic power is not sufficient to meet the needs of the ever-growing production and in 1902, silence once again falls over the valley.

Edouard Aynard, the son-in-law of Raymond de Montgolfier, becomes owner of the abbey in 1906, and undertakes methodically to restore it. He has the two tall chimneys and some 4 000 m_ of industrial buildings demolished. He has the floor of the church excavated to a depth of 80 cm and the east wing of the cloister rebuilt stone by stone.

Thus for a century the Aynards have successively illustrated the same passion for this exceptional abbey.

In 1820, the new purchaser is Louis-Élie de Montgolfier, of the family of the famous Montgolfier brothers, inventors of the hot-air balloon. The next owner, his brother-in-law, Marc Seguin, is also an enthusiastic engineer. At Fontenay, he will build an astronomical observatory.

In the new industrial unit, space is severely lacking. All the rooms are used for the production of paper. The vaulted forge will be no exception.

55

Perspective view of the conventual buildings of Fontenay abbey at the end of the XIIIth century.

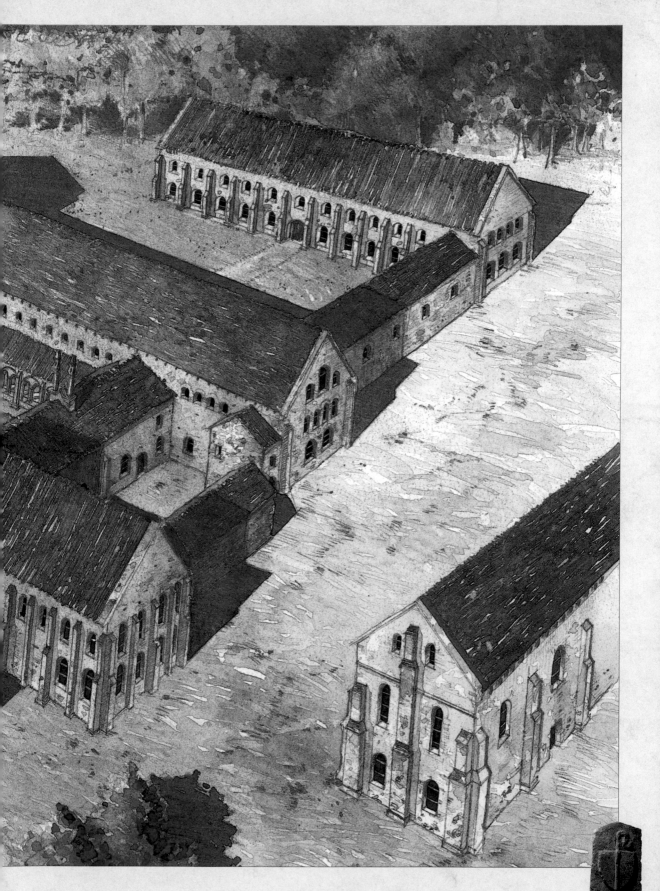

Une tradition d'accueil*

AT THE ABBEY GATE

THE GATE-HOUSE

The monks' abbey is not a hermetically sealed world. To the west of its walls opens the entry to the monastery, the gate-house. Constituting the lodging of the brother gatekeeper, it is surmounted by a floor rebuilt in the XVth century and is built of hewn stone on the outside and of wooden panels framed in masonry inside.

« At the monastery gate shall be placed a wise old man who will know how to receive and how to answer » (*Rule of St. Benedict*, LXVI, 1).

Assigned the task of welcoming guests and distributing alms to poor travellers, the gatekeeper can easily survey the gate-house neighbourhood through a narrow loophole cut in the wall. He is also responsible for closing the heavy gates at nightfall in order to ensure the safety of the community.

A niche is provided under the stairs to the right of the entry porch. From this place, hollowed out in the thickness of the wall, the faithful watchman could easily keep watch over the gatehouse through a quatrefoil opening cut into the bottom of his niche.

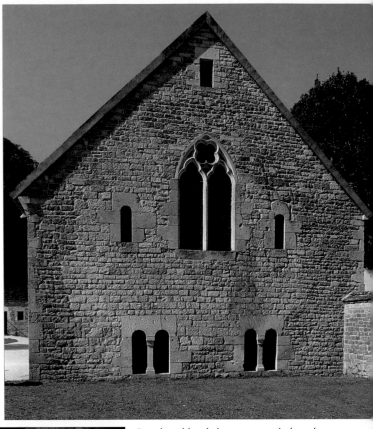

South gable of the strangers' chapel.

Following the elevation of the roof in the XVIIIth century, a small upper floor was constructed above the bakery.

THE STRANGERS CHAPEL

To the left of the gate-house, a XIIIth centur building is built up against the enclosur wall. On the south side, its gable is pierce by a handsome window with two opening in its upper portion, surmounted by a qua drilobate rose. This place was probably th chapel reserved for strangers and wher on their arrival, the abbot came to wis them welcome.

THE BAKERY

A north gable which ends in a semi-spher cal niche and an ancient cylindrical chimne these components betray the presence this very building of the abbey bakery, a though it is quite distant from the kitchen

The floor above the gatekeeper's lodge dates from the XVth century, the epoch when the abbey secured the right to build fortifications against the incessant attacks by pillaging bands and other brigands.

The Welcome

« Like Christ himself, all guests who arrive shall be welcome »

Rule of St. Benedict,
LIII, 1.

THE ABBOT'S LODGINGS

The Limits of the Commendam

The Avignon Popes, in introducing the commendam system, express their desire to control ecclesiastical responsibilities better, but for the Cistercians, this system proves catastrophic. The communities soon no longer enjoy the right of electing their abbot. Appointed by the Pope or by the king, the new abbots are, for the most part, laymen who are being rewarded for good and loyal service, or worldly clergy who are ambitious or corrupt and who behave like the owners of their dependencies, their lands and their personnel, leaving the running of the estates to subordinate officials. Rarely present, these prelates only care about the abbey revenues of which they have charge.

The case of Charles de Sauvebœuf, the ninth commendatory abbot, to the great misfortune of his seven abbeys, including Fontenay, which he holds in commendam, is astonishing. Charles became commendatory abbot when his uncle, Charles d'Escars, Bishop of Langres having resigned from the abbacy, vacated the offices for the new incumbent aged… 13. Since his youth did not permit him to administer the abbeys personally, he initially entrusted their management to an avaricious father. The latter, using the revenues as he wished, only gave to the resident monks what he pleased.

Of the long line of abbots which the abbey received, none held the commendam for such length of time; Charles de Sauvebœuf was abbot from 1614 to 1679, that is to say, for 65 years!

THE DOVECOTE AND THE RED HOUSE

...t two-thirds of its height, the dovecote has a small ...rnice which protected the pigeons from their predators.

...he numerous relaxations of the order rule and the introduction ...f the system of commendatory abbots lead to the adoption of an ...creasingly ostentatious form of decoration which typically adorns ...e « lodgings of the commendatory abbots » of Fontenay. Far re...oved from the stipulations of the Rule of St. Benedict, the abbots ...allow in the luxury of truly lordly lodgings.
...he lodge, located to the east of the cloister not far from the do...cote, was built in the second half of the XVIth century. No fewer ...an thirteen windows on the south side light this stylish home. ...able windows on ornamental roof ridges, a wrought iron bal...ny; the facade possesses a remarkable architectural balance. ...e are here far from the original Cistercian purity, above all when ...is a question of satisfying the commendatory abbots who stay ...t rarely at the abbey.
...front of the abbey church, a mere few steps away, rises the mas...ve tower of a lovely dovecote. Dating back presumably to the ...IIth century, it is a reminder of the « droit de pigeon » reserved ...the abbey, the authorisation to breed these birds whose flesh ...ll be tasted with pleasure by important visitors.

The name Red House suggests the colour of the plastering.

61

THE TERRACOTTA TILES

Conclusion

Tiles with inset motif.

Tiles with inset motif.

Tiles with relief decoration.

THE DEVELOPMENT OF DECORATED PAVING

Though excluding sculpture and paintings from Cistercian buildings, the Order does tolerate paving, provided that it consists of stone or terracotta tiles without any decoration. Bernard de Clairvaux, in his *Apology*, is categorical : « Without mosaics composed of figures of angels and saints, characters on whom one spits and whom one treads underfoot, without differently coloured tiles ». At most, tiles can exhibit geometrical forms, engraved in the earth before it has been hardened.

The use of decorated and enamelled tiles became very widespread throughout Burgundy from the beginning of the XIIIth century onwards, and it is not surprising that when the rule underwent some relaxation, Fontenay abbey developed the use of these tiles with numerous ornamental combinations.

At Fontenay, these tiles covered a large part of the choir and church, as can be seen from a procedural text dated August 10, 1752. This ancient text gives an account of the proce-

...o-tone tiles with inlaid decoration.

...ure between the monks and the adjudicators on the ...bject of repairs to be carried out in about 1750. The ...vel of the choir having been raised, the decorated ...es were transported to the cloister where they were ...ed to pave two galleries. It is there that they were ...und in very large numbers at the time restoration ...ork undertaken by the Aynard family at the beginning ... the XXth century...

...ERAMIC TECHNIQUES

... these relaxations lead the general council of the ...apter to call on a number of abbeys to observe the ...le and to order abbots to demolish the offending ...vings which, because of their whimsical motifs, were ...nsidered « curious and frivolous ».

...hat are these motifs ? Stylised drawings of monsters, ... lions or griffins, subjects which bear witness to the ...axation.

...ese decorated pavings represent a break with the first ...stercian tiles which are, for the most part, designed to

form rose motifs by their four-by-four arrangement. These tiles are of variable size, between 8 and 15 centimetres. Some bear a simple design, carved in the clay whilst it is still malleable, and are covered with a black, yellow or brick red glaze. Others are decorated according to the technique used in Burgundy in the XIIIth century; the design is carved to a shallow depth using a stamp and then filled with coloured pastes which contrast sharply with the darker background. The glaze of these designs, often less resistant than that of the background, has suffered severely from the passage of feet.

The majority of the tiles found are manufactured in the abbeys, by hand, by the monks themselves. However, to attribute, on the basis of these tiles, the origin of the technique of mediæval tile-making to Cistercian monks... Taking their inspiration from local products, they established their own production, achieving great skill in the use of ceramic products and earths of various colours. Some even placed their know-how at the disposal of strangers to the order.

...o-tone tiles with inlaid decoration.

Extract from the Apology about Paving

« Why are the images of the saints in the paving which we tread underfoot not respected ? Often, one spits in the mouth of an angel and sometimes passers-by deface the face of a saint. Even if one has no respect for the sanctity of these images, one should at least spare the beauty of the colours. Why embellish what will be ruined on the first day ? Why paint by hand what will necessarily be obliterated by feet ? Of what use are beautiful paintings which are exposed to soiling by constant dust ? In a word, of what use are all these things to the poor, the monks and men of the spirit ? Unless one borrows [...] the words of the prophet: "Lord, I have loved the beauty of your house and the dwelling-place of your glory." (Ps. XXXV, 8). »

Extract from *Apologia ad Guillelmum*, 1123-1125, Bernard de Clairvaux.

AROUND THE ABBEY

THE MUNIÈRES PITS

In the Middle Ages, the lords of Montbard granted the Fontenay monks numerous rights to exploit the iron ore found in the neighbouring woods, particularly in a place called Les Munières a few hundred metres from the abbey.

Although these grants are effective, they nevertheless do not mean that the mines are accessible; the deposits generally remaining to be discovered, developed and then exploited.

Good yields are ensured, as the iron content of the ore brought up by the miner's efforts is over 50 %.

ON SITE

A clearly indicated walking path (red markings) makes it possible to explore the site. Here the visitor will find abundant information on the process of iron extraction.

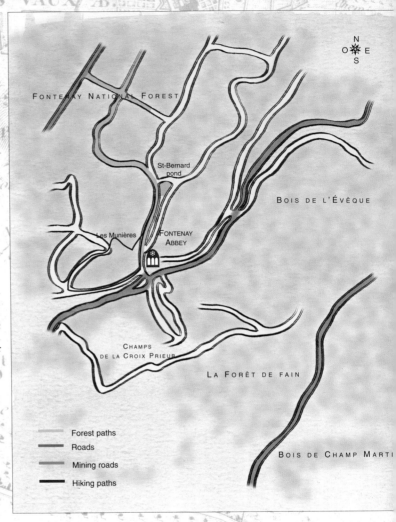

FONTENAY NATIONAL FOREST

St-Bernard pond

BOIS DE L'ÉVÊQUE

Les Munières

FONTENAY ABBEY

CHAMPS DE LA CROIX PRIEUR

LA FORÊT DE FAIN

BOIS DE CHAMP MARTI

— Forest paths
— Roads
— Mining roads
— Hiking paths

Ex-libris (Bibliothèque nationale, Latin ms. 2436, fol. 126 r
Customary Fontenay ex-libris label, recalling that
Cistercian monasteries are dedicated to the Virg